MIXTURAO

AND OTHER POEMS

MIXTURAO
AND OTHER POEMS

TATO LAVIERA

Arte Público Press
Houston, Texas

Mixturao and Other Poems is made possible through grants from the City of Houston through the Houston Arts Alliance, and by the Exemplar Program, a program of Americans for the Arts in Collaboration with the LarsonAllen Public Services Group, funded by the Ford Foundation.

Recovering the past, creating the future

Arte Público Press
University of Houston
452 Cullen Performance Hall
Houston, Texas 77204-2004

Cover design by Mora Des!gn
Cover art by Roberto Juarez, "Sun Woman, 1982"

Laviera, Tato
Mixturao and Other Poems / by Tato Laviera.
p. cm.
ISBN 978-1-55885-524-3 (alk. paper)
1. Puerto Ricans—Poetry 2. Ethnicity—United States—Poetry.
I. Title
PS3562.A849M59 2008
811′.54—dc22 2008015946
CIP

∞ The paper used in this publication meets the requirements of the American National Standard for Information Sciences—Permanence of Paper for Printed Library Materials, ANSI Z39.48-1984.

8 9 0 1 2 3 4 5 6 7 10 9 8 7 6 5 4 3 2 1

Contents

Hombres

Vecindario

Acknowledgments

I would like to acknowledge the editorial assistance of Bess White, Sonia Pérez, Elizabeth García, Masaia Yuma, Paula Acosta, and Anna White.

I am grateful to my literary colleagues, William Luis and Stephanie Álvarez Martínez for their support.

I dedicate Mixturao and Other Poems *to*
Dr. Nicolás Kanellos for his years of dedication
and excellence in promoting Latino literature.

I also dedicate this book to
my grandchild and grandnephews,
Kayden Laviera-Gog, Simeon Joseph Hargrave,
and Grayson Sánchez.

Tato Laviera: Mix(ing) t(hro)u(gh)ou(t)

Tato Laviera is certainly one of those rare, original, and gifted poets who comes along once in a great while. He is the voice and consciousness of a community that continues to strive for a dream that has eluded generations of people who have endured the cold and inhospitable, wintery environment where they reside.

As the perennial witness to the unfolding of societal events, Laviera smells, sees, listens, tastes, and touches all that surrounds him. But Laviera does not have to use all of his senses to understand and chronicle the various rhythms of his society; his spirit and heart guide his pen as he moves swiftly and imperceptibly from the bottom of a maze of uncertainty, confusion, and despair and rises to access a spiritual path that informs and enlightens those who believe and follow. For, indeed, Laviera's poetry is political, cultural, sensual, but also highly spiritual and religious.

This prophet speaks with one voice but, more correctly, with many voices and sounds. Through him, we hear the music of the barrios, of children playing and people singing, yelling, preaching, rapping, whispering, lovemaking, cursing, crying, and laughing. However, we also listen to the sounds of people walking, cars passing, a door closing, a can opening. If we pay attention closely, we may even take notice of other sounds emanating from such unlikely places as an apartment wall, pavement, empty courtyard, chain-link fence, fire escape, and lamppost. We can clearly hear some of his characters speak, like Can Picker ("I am a twentieth century welfare recipient"), Preacher ("god bless sister sarah"), Guerrilla ("we would not have to pick up the gun"), Melao ("i am a jíbaro"), Machista ("la, tú sabes, tipa esa, me tiene, lo oíste,"), Barrio ("el inglés / se deforma / con el / calor de / tu cultura"), and fetus, Jesús Papote ("Mami Mami push push i'm coming out celestial barkings").

Laviera's poetry speaks to one neighborhood and to many neighborhoods: the Nuyorican and the Cuban, Dominican, Chicano, Mexican, Panamanian, African American, and others. The reader is exposed to the concerns of a broader mainstream society that is common to all. In "lady liberty" of *Mainstream Ethics*,[1] we take notice of the symbol of freedom and the sounds of those commemorating the bicentennial of the United States. While everyone is engaged in the festivities, few observe her decomposed body and even less remember her real significance, now lost in time. In a moment of despair, Lady Liberty awakens and voices her discontent for those who have been left behind:

> if you touch me, touch ALL of my people
> who need attention and societal repair,
> give the tired and the poor
> the same attention, AMERICA,
> touch us ALL with liberty,
> touch us ALL with liberty. (7)

With *Mixturao and Other Poems*, Tato Laviera returns to poetry after a twenty-year absence (*Mainstream Ethics* was published by Arte Público Press in 1988). Though Laviera has dedicated much of the past decades to teaching, poetry readings, and writing plays, he has never abandoned the art form that has brought him international recognition. For Laviera, poetry is everywhere, in his apartment building, as he walks the streets, listens to music, sits in a restaurant, rides the subway, and converses with friends. Poetry is also present in his plays and the voices of his characters.

With his latest collection of poetry, Laviera situates himself more firmly in an in-between state, known to him throughout his life, which has provided him with a sense of comfort, identity, and a strong voice. Except that now he embraces it with conviction. As a prophet or visionary, contemporary social, political, economic, and historical

[1] (Houston: Arte Público P, 1988).

developments in the United States have confirmed what he has always known: the mixing of languages, cultures, races, social classes, music, and histories is an inevitable consequence when people of diverse backgrounds meet and interact in the same adopted country.

Divided into Folklores, Fronteras, Mujeres, Hombres, and Vecindario, each section reflects the overall thematic conveyed by the book's title, *Mixturao*, that is, a mixture or *mezcla* or any type of blending. The word itself, in Spanglish, graphically reproduces its own meaning; Laviera proposes an English title but pronounces or writes it in Spanish, thus signifying a "Mixture Throughout" every aspect of the collection.

The essence of *Mixturao* is contained in the beginning poems. "Nideaquinideallá" reflects a hybrid, hyphenated experience, or in between state, perhaps incorporating both, "deaquiydeallá," but also negating it, "nideaquinideallá." The title is in Spanish, but the poem is written in English and Spanish and combines both languages, because neither language by itself is sufficient to convey the richness of a diverse, multicultural experience. Languages tend to homogenize cultural expressions and demand an allegiance to a singular identity as defined by the dominant culture. For this reason, Laviera mixes the two languages and creates an in-between state so as not to belong to either one of them, which paradoxically offers him a sense of belonging in a society of exclusion. He is not from one place or another; rather, he is from no place and refuses to be attached or associated with a particular national or cultural identity. Instead of being from one barrio, town, city, or country, he is from here and there, but his newfound name is from nowhere, nideaquinideallá. "My first name is de aquí . . . " "My middle name is de allá . . . " "my last new latest name: / nideaquínideallá / impossible to blend / impossible to categorize / impossible to analyze / impossible to synthesize . . . " (4-6). His name emerges from a concrete and complex social and linguistic condition.

"Español" explains the poet's conflictive relationship with what some would consider to be his mother tongue. It expresses his resolve to distance and even reject it, which, from the speaker's point of view, has betrayed him. However, it also conveys his inability to do so completely. As Spanish migrated, the language was brought to other cultures, which it branded or redefined with its own sense of value that was not necessarily applicable to the new environment. So from the fragments a different language, with a Spanish core, emerged as a new one. In so doing, the changes threatened the old order, as well as the guardians of the language:

> metiéndole miedo a tu real academia
> española cucándote con millones de
> palabras continentales trabalenguas
> enmixturadas cocinándose en asuntos . . . (20)

The old "sacred" Spanish cannot speak to the new reality, which materializes from very specific conditions that include the cultures and languages of other people. Spanish is Spain's last symbol of its imperial power, the same one that exploited the natural resources used to construct and sustain the Spanish Empire. The poetic voice considers the mixture of the language he employs, evident in the poem, to be another variation of the many dialects spoken, and is justified by its own traditions.

In spite of the speaker's opposition to using an archaic linguistic form to express another reality not envisioned by the traditions of that language, he recognizes the contradiction in which he lives. Though he questions Spanish, he is also aware that the language is a part of who he is. Spanish changes and regenerates and is a product of other mixtures, and with time produces dialects with their own particularities and literatures, which speak to the experiences of specific linguistic communities. He does not and cannot reject Spanish totally, since he considers it "half of my lengua;" the other part is conveyed by the first five lines of the stanza and repeated in the first three English words of the previously quoted line, which in number seem to overshadow the Spanish "lengua." The balance is reestablished in the last three Spanish lines of the poem: "qué tragedia / qué contra / dic ci ón" (21).

There are two other poems that demonstrably continue the linguistic debate: "Spanglish" and "Bilingüe." In the first, the poetic voice is conscious of creating a system of signification, derived from the coming together of two cultures, with its own system of rules. This is not something that happens haphazardly, but has its own structure and meaning. Spanglish, as a bilingual and bicultural system, has all the linguistic markers associated with any language, including English, and should be accepted as such.

In "Bilingüe," Laviera resorts to the Spanish language that is half his, as described in the poem "Español," and writes a bilingual poem, in which both Spanish and English are reproduced as standard languages. The Spanish is taken from a popular song, "Olas y arenas," recorded by the Puerto Rican singer Sylvia Rexach, who met with an untimely death. If the left column reproduces, with some variation, Rexach's song, the right side is not a literal translation of the song, as the title "Bilingüe" conveys, but an interpretation of the song or an amplification of it. In this poem, Tato embraces Spanish and Hispanic culture through the words of Rexach and unites or mixes his voice with hers, thus producing a bilingual composition, a duet if you wish, by Rexach and Laviera. But this bilingual poem, which starts in English ("exploring and dissecting"), has as its foundation Spanish (Rexach's song). The poem, inspired by the mother tongue, is expressed or interpreted in the column to the right in standard English, and slowly converts into a truly bilingual poem in which Spanish and English are intermixed as the words are placed side by side. So the poem can be read many ways. First, you can proceed vertically, reading the first column, starting with the introductory stanza, written in English and Spanish, and the latter continues with Rexach's song. This reading persists with the second column, written first in English and then in both languages. Second, the poem can be read horizontally. In this reading you, again, begin with the introductory stanza, and continue with the first line of the song, then proceed to the second column, with the interpretation in English, thus mixing Rexach's poem with Laviera's words, one appearing to speak to the other. However, toward the end, in the last three lines, the two voices appear to harmonize as both singer and poet speak to each other in the same language.

Rexach's song is romantic in nature and corresponds to another theme found in Laviera's poetry, most evident in the section Mujeres. In "Bilingüe," Rexach compares herself to a lonely grain of sand wanting to be touched by the waves, like the other grains she envies.

However, a big wave arrives and believing that this time she will be consumed, the wave recedes and disappears among the others. Laviera's response is a meeting of sorts. If she has waited for the wave, then he has arrived and merges with her, physically and metaphorically. He embraces Rexach, her poem, the Spanish language, and produces another symbolic representation of Puerto Rico:

i receive your luscious lips
buscándote borinquen
your cinnamon-powdered
tongue mi tierra
somos siete millones
en múltiples
fronteras lingüísticas. (28)

Though Puerto Rico is a small island, Puerto Ricans live in many different places. They carry their language and culture wherever they go and intermix their Spanish with other languages.

"Español," "Spanglish," "Bilingue," and "Nideaquinideallá" culminate in "Mixturao," (29-30) which gives title to the collection. It represents a communal expression against the forces that produce and promote linguistic and political isolation. The "I" in the previous poems is transformed into a strong majority of "we," present in the opening line of every stanza: "we who engage in," "we who integrate," "we who grassroots," "we who create continental music," "we who are at peace in continental." This plural pronoun is further reflected with the plural possessive "our," "so enter our multi-lingual," in the last stanza, which embraces the continental richness of languages, races, music, and overwhelms the interrogative "who are you, English / telling me, 'Speak only English / or die'." The structure is repeated at the end of almost every stanza, that is, at the bottom, as if crushing the English or sustaining the weight of an overwhelmingly diverse society. "Who are you English," defined as intransigent, holding fast to outdated modalities, expresses itself in worn out clichés, such as "'speak only English or die' / 'love it or leave it'." However, in the final stanza, the poetic voice reaches out to U.S. isolationism, paranoia, and narrow-mindedness and welcomes it into the community of "partners." In this stanza the speaker reveals himself through the "I," expressed as a singular but with a plural content, with strength and determination, confronts the "who are you, English" and with a resounding voice identifies himself as embodying "continental 'MIXTURAO'."

It should be evident that language is essential for Laviera. In a 1989 interview with this critic, Laviera refers to the structure of his poetry and the use of Spanish in his writings: "Everything is structured so that *nadie me joda*. I have published 198 poems: 60 percent of the poems are totally in English, 20 percent of them are totally in Spanglish, and the remaining 20 percent I write in total Spanish . . . . So politically I have to write Spanish and English to cover all the grounds of my people. *No quiero pleito con la gente mía*."[2]

In his previous works, Laviera made sure to set aside a section for poems in Spanish. *Mixturao* represents a departure from that position, since he presently embraces more enthusiastically Spanglish, or a mixturao of Spanish and English. In so doing, he situates himself in a third space, as described by Gloria Anzaldúa's *Borderlands/La Frontera* or Homi K Bhabha's *Location of Culture*.[3] But for Laviera it is expressed or achieved by embracing linguistic, cultural, and thematic combinations. The transition between the past and the present can be further seen in his emphasis on "hispano," of *Mainstream Ethics*, and "Latino," of *Mixturao*. In the first, located in the section corresponding to poems written in Spanish, he underscored the traditions of Spanish-speaking countries, as expressed in music: vals, vallenato, samba, merengueadas, ranchera, mambo, salsa, plena, bolero, cha cha chá, cumbia, bomba, guaracha . . . . In the second, "hispano" gives way to "Latino," expressed in a poem written exclusively in English. Whereas "hispano" emphasized the Hispanic language, culture, and traditions, "Latino" is a communal acceptance of the adopted environment that produces a new and hybrid culture, based on the coming together of differences.

---

[2] "From New York to the World: An Interview With Tato Laviera," *Callaloo* 15.4 (Autumn 1992): 1028.

[3] Gloria Anzaldúa, *Borderlands: The New Mestiza* (San Francisco: Aunt Lute, 1987); Homi K Bhabha, *The Location of Culture* (London: Routledge, 1994).

The acceptance of New York City and the rejection of the romantic return to Puerto Rico, as seen, for example, in René Marqués *La carreta*,[4] was already present in Laviera's own *La Carreta Made a U-Turn*,[5] and demonstrably evident in Miguel Piñero's "A Lower East Side Poem."[6] In the latter, Piñero understands that Puerto Rico is no longer the place he desires; instead, he wants to die in the Lower East Side—thus the popular refrain: "then scatter my ashes thru / the Lower East Side"—even though the space he has chosen houses some of the most questionable and sinister elements of society (prostitutes, junkies, pimps, thieves) with which he also identifies. Like Piñero, Laviera embraces that same environment. But, unlike his fellow poet, Laviera sees it differently. For him, it is full of hope and optimism, described with words like "win," "ambitions," aspirations," "Mobility," "advancement," and "Healthy-looking razas" (7). Of course, the struggle is not easy, and one must continue to be vigilant.

Of the poems contained in *Mixturao*, less than a handful, like "Riqueña Hip-Hop," which celebrates the Puerto Rican motherland, are written completely in Spanish. All the other dominant Spanish poems contain some words in English. Laviera does not abandon Spanish, but these poems are few and far between, no longer set aside in a separate section, but are interspersed thoughtout the collection and sprinkled with English and Spanglish. This is evident in "El Difunto," a poem that reads like a chronicle and a prayer, since the Lord's Prayer is reproduced in Spanish in a separate column to the right of the poem. In fact, there is a relationship between the two, not only because both respond to religious practices, but also because each stanza corresponds to a line in the prayer and both are thirty in number. The poetic voice refuses to enter the funeral, knowing that all those in attendance are hypocrites, including the deceased's so-called daughter. In some respects, the poetic voice is reminiscent of Edgardo Rodríguez Juliá's narrator, who chronicles the burial of Cortijo, which, according to the narrator, had its share of dramatic hypocrites, including the famed Ismaelo.[7] If Rodríguez Juliá writes his chronicle

[4] (Río Piedras, P.R.: Editorial Cultural, 1969).

[5] (Arte Público P, 1979).

[6] "A Lower East Side Poem," in Faythe Turner, *Puerto Rican Writers at Home in the USA* (Seattle: Open Hand Publishing, 1991), 131.

[7] See: *El entierro de Cortijo* (Río Piedras, P.R.: Ediciones Huracán, 1991).

for posterity, the poetic voice shows more familiarity with the deceased; he stands outside the church, witnesses the event, and fulfills his promise, to close the casket so that his friend does not have to see any of those predictable cultural performances.

Closest to Spanish is "Callejerismos," a poem associated with the gossip in the street. The poem, narrated as a stream of consciousness, contains a few words in English, such as "complaint," "boring," "equal opportunity," and "number one" (57-59). The topic of the poem is music, and the speaker proposes the merengue as the quintessential music. In so doing, he enters into a debate regarding music in the Caribbean and among Caribbean people living in the United States. Whereas Cubans claim to be the originators of Salsa, Puerto Ricans are the best arrangers, and Nuyoricans are the Kings of Rap. However, as to be expected, Cuba emerges as a problematic subject, and the speaker spreads rumors that Miami Cuban American musicians, like Gloria Estefan, boycott Puerto Rico because Andy Montañez visited the renowned troubadour, Pablo Milanés, in Cuba.

If in a previous period there was a Caribbean camaraderie, the speaker attacks Cubans, Dominicans, and Puerto Rican music, and finds common ground with people of color, hybrid cultures in the United States, and Nuyoricans and Tex-Mex, as he associates Selena and J Lo, but also African Americans:

> . . . pero Selena la del tex-mex era la
> más chula del mundo ésa tenía capacidad de
> competir con la J Lo los nuyorican bailan
> como los prietos . . . (58)

The speaker finds value in the bachata, which originated in the rural communities of the Dominican Republic. Some will continue to debate which is the best dance or music, but the speaker proclaims the merengue as the music of Latin American, even though it began in the Dominican Republic. It is a natural type of music, with natural dance movements, because we are born dancing merengue: "porque uno nace bailando merengue . . . " (58).

Race, tangentially present in "Callejerismos," with African Americans and Dominican bachata and merengue, has been a constant and necessary metaphor for Laviera's poetry. Though not perceptible in every poem, Laviera's vision of race speaks to its presence in both

Hispanic and U.S. societies. It may not be coincidental that these societies, separated by language, geography, and culture, share the same or similar positions regarding blacks and the place they occupy in their respective societies. "Tesis de Negreza," a poem written in Spanish and inspired by Víctor Manuel Vega's doctorate dissertation,[8] takes issue with Bobby Capó's popular song, "Negro bembón." Ironically, Rafael Cortijo and Ismael Rivera, who werc both Afro-Puerto Ricans, popularized the composition. "Negro bembón" is one of a few songs that celebrate the murder of blacks; another one is Gilberto Monroig's "El negrito ñénguere."[9] In his, Capó makes fun of blacks and their thick lips. However, the title and subtext recall Luis Palés Matos' negrista poems.

As with "Español" and Sylvia Rexach's "Olas de arenas," Laviera's "Tesis de Negreza" reproduces at the beginning of each stanza a line of "Negro bembón," followed by a response or commentary, which gains in intensity as the song and poem unfold. If the song describes the killing of the Thick Lipped Black, as a translation of the title suggests, the investigative officer questions why the culprit killed the dearly beloved black man. The culturally acceptable and humorous, but here offensive and shocking, answer pertains to his labial characteristics: "yo lo maté por ser tan BEMBÓN" (24). The officer, who himself is black, rolls up his lip and hides this racial maker, perhaps fearing not so much a similar outcome, because the killer is under custody, but because of social and racial condemnation. Laviera takes issue with the response; in his poem, the officer is not evasive and uncovers the racism behind the remarks:

> "el guardia escondió la lengua y le dijo"
> soy *niche* para insultarte cuando me insultes
> para confrontarte cuando tu ignorancia
> desigualdad escupe estereotipos
> soy *lobo* voy a sacar la bemba patriótica
> colectiva humana cuando me respetes
> amistosamente. (24)

---

[8] Víctor Manuel Vega, "An Analysis of Centrality of the Latino of African Descent: Understanding Afrocentric Agency in a Selected Segment of Contemporary Representative Latinos of African Descent," diss., Temple U, 2001.

[9] Guaracha (Seeco, 1957).

Unlike the other officer, this one is proud of his African ancestry, which he shares with others throughout the continents of the Americas. He embraces all of the derogatory colonial classifications whites attribute to non whites: "grifo," "mestizo," "moreno," "morisco," "moyeto," "negro pardo," "quinterón," "retinto," "saltoatrás," "tente en el aire," "torno atrás," "zambo," and others. In addition, he turns societal values upside down and shows himself, who according to society is racially inferior, to be more dignified than the white perpetrator. Not only does the officer reveal that blacks are an inherent component of the nation and the national, but he leaves the door open for possible reconciliation and friendship with his adversary. He now displays his lips with pride and sense of identity.

"Southwest Border Trucos" emphasizes a connection with other hybrid cultures in the United States. In so doing, Laviera documents one of the most sensitive issues confronting U.S. society, the most recent trend in migration, as Mexicans find their way north to New York City, once hailed as the largest Puerto Rican and later Dominican communities outside of their countries of origin. There is a similarity between the Mexican and the Puerto Rican experiences, each dominated by their most powerful neighbor. The occupations produced waves of migrations, and many abandoned their place of residence to find work in the north. But in recent years workers from the interior of Mexico are prohibited from passing onto lands that once belonged to that nation-state. In this respect, there are differences between Puerto Ricans and Mexicans: the former travel north unencumbered as U.S. citizens, and the latter do the same, however, by outsmarting the Immigration and Naturalization Services.

Crossing the border responds to a cultural movement that existed before there was a border, when the land belonged to Mexico, and present-day immigrants continue the migratory traditions known to their forefathers. Currently, they resort to the most inventive ways to reach the land once so familiar to them. The poem ends with the following stanza:

> But ultimately sabemos que *Nuevo México,*
> *Texas, California, Arizona y Colorado*
> Are always *nuestras tierras.* We come-enter *a*
> *Nuestro gusto, con ganas. Estas*
> *Fronteras son mexicanas, de México, compadrito.*

Ajúa, cholo, chale, ese no la chingues.
Canta, gallito cross without concern
Nuevo México es terreno de Pancho Villa. (10)

For the speaker, Mexico and the Southwest are not divided by a border and continue to be an extension of the same land.

Just as Laviera chronicled the bicentennial of his adopted homeland through the voice of Ms. Liberty, he does the same with a more recent event that shook the foundations of this most powerful nation in the world. In "Innocence," he records the devastating events of 9/11, which launched the United States into a war in Afghanistan, and subsequently Iraq. During that tragedy in which "Perpetrators murdered over / 3,000 civilians point blank!:"

looking for miracles, rescue turned to
recovery and removal, ash-laden carnage,
evaporated humans, particles remnants
of 1,000,000 body parts. (67)

The catastrophic event produced a unifying effect seen only a few times in U.S. history; everyone set aside differences, united in sympathy, became instant patriots, and supported the cause they shared.

Indeed, this was the day the United States lost its "Innocence," though there were other moments, such as the invasion of Pearl Harbor and the deaths of John F. Kennedy, his brother Robert Kennedy and, of course, Martin Luther King. While the poetic voice understands the patriotic feeling this action provoked, the strongest nation on Earth, with all its resources, was helpless at the hands of a few terrorists. United States might and power were imperceptible, and the country was unable to protect its citizens. And just as the attack on Pearl Harbor necessitated a governmental response, the speaker recognizes that "Now the nation must flex its muscles" (70). Nevertheless, the strongest reaction originates from the collective "We," of which the speaker is a part. In fact, the poetic voice assumes the consciousness of a nation that must proceed with humility and honesty and recognize its mistakes. Perhaps, "We" fired or attacked first by imposing our democratic system on people of different cultures, by exporting aspects of U.S. society that are indeed offensive to others.

So the "We" in Laviera's poem becomes a paradoxical or plural "we." On the one hand, "We will investigate e-mail;" on the other, "We must not become / vigilantes and discriminators" (71), for all those predispositions undermine the very nature of the society "we" consider to be home. "We" have lost our innocence and the liberties for which our country stood. There is no question regarding the poetic voice's outrage, especially with his accusation, "Terrorist you are called!" (73). The attack was not only against the United States, but also the world. In addition, it was against the children, who represent the future, and it is for their sake that the speaker pleas for a change, "Reform your hatred," in the name of the mystical leaders of Christian and Muslim religions, but more tangibly in the name of Love, considered the most powerful force. Whereas Allah and God each are mentioned once, the "children" are repeated twice and so are the final lines of the poem, "Love knows no compromise!" (73).

Mixturao is the voice of a new generation of people of Hispanic descent, that is, people whose parents were born and raised in Hispanic countries and later migrated to the United States. Their children, who were born or raised in the United States, are more affected by the cultural conditions of their adopted country. They combine the language and culture of their parents with those of their present homeland to produce a new one that combines the two.[10] With *Mixturao*, Laviera steps forward to lead a future generation of writers and readers into the promised land, not the mythical one reserved for the afterlife, but the one that is currently unfolding in our lifetime, the one that accepts differences, is proud of its hybrid culture, respects people of all races, and includes Spanglish and anything else that produces a Mixturao.

William Luis
Chancellor's Professor of Spanish
Vanderbilt University
April 2008

[10] I contend that Hispanic writers are those who are born, raised, and educated in their native countries and later emigrated or were forced to flee to the United States, where they continue to write in Spanish. Latino authors are those who are born or raised and educated in the United States and for the most part write in English. For more information see *Dance Between Two Cultures: Latino Caribbean Literature Written in the United States* (Nashville: Vanderbilt UP, 1997.)

Folklores

Word

(for the bard Jorge Brandon)

"Poetry was meant to be heard
Poetry was meant to be read"
Indomitable companions
Interactions
Simultaneously
Quivering reader
Fullest sensorial
Written realizations

"Poetry was meant to be read"
Silent reading internality
Between eye-of-I
Involved in total
Self-absorption
Capturing intellect
Treasures pleasures
Orgasmic intonations
Dignified silence
Intimately touching
At innermost

"Poetry was meant to be heard"
Spoken word
Oral transmission
Listener exposed to
Vocabularies
Ear's timpani
Exploration vowels
Consonants physically
Muscling personal
Voices integrated
Stimulated tonalities

So read deep in
So read out loud
Drench two communions
Enjoy inventive historical
All-time coup d'gras.

nideaquinideallá

de qué I know yo sí sé
backnforth here soy de aquí
regreso dicen y qué what
aterricé o acá o allá

my first name is de aquí
my last name is de allá
my last name is nideaquinideallá
yet-to-be defined
evolucionario hybrid

backnforth here soy de aquí
cannot be defined
cannot be categorized
cannot be pasteurizao
cannot be homogenizao

what's my new name?
¿cómo me dicen?
regreso a mi tierra nativa
me llaman y qué what
les contesto somos
we are the children
immigrant/migrantes
our madres cutting
blood crowns entering
fronteras wired fences
nuestros padres wrinkled
foreheads peso of dollar-
an-hour miseria
our uncles and tías
flesh-skinned manos
see-through cemented
tenements hard-core trabajo
mis hermanos and sisters
open-preyed borders
societal disasters

de qué i know yo sí sé
in my yet-to-be defined
birthplace homeland
dual citizenship accusations
indignations differentiations
pesadillas de callos
intellectual displacements
transplanting raíces
aquí no allá yes aquí allá
backnforth no sé si maybe
in between schizophrenia
cultural ataques in all
directions hip-hopping
nightmares paralyzing
incertidumbres frenéticas

aterricé o acá o allá
child of western hemispheric
creations ancestral inheritors
not knowing past three
previous generations
my boricua sobrenombre
original by parent's birth
caribbean by folklore
hispanic by culture
nuyorican by geographic
migrational displacements
latino by mutual promotion
urban by modern necessity
offspring of indigenous dialectics
too many hats to wear
too little time to square
qué vida what a life

I'm in the usa of america
and in us of a, you suffer
insignias of apathy
prejuicio subtle racism
minority status

us of a, you suffer
watching our nation invading other nations without an invitation

My middle name is de allá
constant anti-nuyorican
anti-latino born wedlock
on u.s. soil bilingual
problemas not me anymore
we in all of us ustedes
siempre malnombrándonos
we fight not to be brainwashed
so se acabó el relajo
stop mental disenfranchisement
my last new latest name:

nideaquinideallá
impossible to blend
impossible to categorize
impossible to analyze
impossible to synthesize
our guerrilla cultural camouflage
survival linguistic construction
at emergency moment's notice
complex afirmaciones parametric
principles fermenting
secretive universal
garabatopandegato
continental yearnings
complex jeringonza
de mi hablar

nideaquinideallá
escríbelo junto
sin letra mayúscula
gracias

Latino

We are from here
Bred to win
Family's ambitions
Aspirations upward
Mobility adelante
Centers of advancement
Alluring mixtures
Healthy-looking razas
Societal experimenters
Multi-rhythmic embracers
Musically popping top charts
Blending gracefully
Limited economic
Power operators
Struggling at bottom
Ladder entry points
Concluding that our pride
Cannot settle for crumbs
Hand-me-downs so
We don't open our eyes
We never close them.

Southwest Border Trucos

When you see *mexicanos*
Progressing in your *barrios*
Working for los *coreanos*
Cooking for all New Yorkers
Pressing laundry garments
Winning international marathons
Receiving two dollars an hour
Undocumented non-card misery
Remember they represent
A free independent nation
Thirty million largest Latino population
Nachos, salsa, burritos, guacamole
Mariachi, national folklore Taco Bell.

When you see *mexicanos ilegales*
Selling fruit and flowers in all kinds of weather
Bow your head
To a formidable free nation
To a great Latino people
To a great *Hispano* nation
La voz de Aztlán speaking in deed!

"Estoy celebrando la migra deftness, *Chuy,*
Pues ahorita te cuento, cuate,
Somos five-hundred-year-old *dueños*
Of United States territories, *pinche güey.*
We have over fifty percent *español*
Linguistic ownership west of the Mississippi, *ese.*
We owned the west-*oeste* before Thirteen
Colonies *gringos*' imperialist western expansion
Militaristically illegally annexed us, *carnal.*

"Pues, ahorita te cuento, compadre.
La cellular walkie-talkie ten-four security
Alguaciles boundary between El Paso, Texas y

Juárez, México los americanos protestan que la
Bandera mexicana scaling *cincuenta pies de*
Altura y cincuenta pies de ancha dominates all
Billboards leading to *el aeropuerto de la*
Borde entre Estados Unidos la ten-four *nos*
Vigilan our illegal entry so that we don't
Cross into our original *fronteras* from our
Squatter housing.

"Qué cabrones ignorantes.
Nosotros somos
Lifetime experts of *Río Grande historia, vato.*
Somos administradores of *El Río* Certification
Notary Services international consortium, *carnal.*

"Pues, ahorita te cuento, madre,
Las mujeres de la noche conocen the hourly
Shift of *americanos* patroling *su enchilada*
Lunch breaks and the *gringos'* eight-men rosters, *mano.*
Las mujeres occupy leadership positions in
Counter-intelligence. They also monitor their
Boozing *hábitos en las tavernas, hombre.*

"*Nosotros,* daily sponsors of buy-one-get-two
Tequilas paid by the council of *cruzados*,
Save ten percent of our underground
Collection fees for supporting services of
Young *mexicano* undergraduate students at
UT El Paso and New Mexico Aggies. They
Submit to us general profiles of *los* rednecks
Hired to arrest us, *padre*.

"The civil servants are non-college upper-lower-
Class up to their necks with installment payments.
They cash their checks en *las tavernas,* are uneducated
On budget plans, and are abusive of spouses unattentive to
Children's growth. *Son simples brutos* generally they
Only capture us asleep or *borrachos, qué chingadera.*

"*También tenemos* computer charts. We know they are
Slow *por las mañanitas cuando no hay tráfico. Uno
Cruza feliz* the border. Supervisor *sabe de las
Redadas de la* ICE *buscando las drogas las veinte y
Cinco mil maneras creativas* to smuggle *pero el
Teniente* Ellae likes *las prostitutas* especially
La Madame Emma La Pollona singing *con
Mariachis mientras* she stripteases. *En la
Oficina* we make Xerox copies of their weekly
Raids usually occurring after five for overtime
Benefits, *mi hermano.*

"But, what the hell, *carajo*, we cross *el
Río Grande veinte y cuatro horas* a day *a comer los*
McDonalds at university pizzerias, *macho*. We
Offer daily tours to potential immigrants. *Les
Llenamos los papeles del* Social Security. We have
Cincuenta maneras to penetrate backnforth, *primo*.

"*Le metemos* sleeping pills *en las fajitas de guacamole,
Adobamos el* lime *de las coronas con* horny ingredients
*Picantes para que se les paren los chingues.
Rentando cuartos*, we press their
Uniformes with green pepper *ajillos calientes
Pa' que se rasquen las nalgas* to complain and bitch with the
Sun's heat and leave *media hora tempranito, carnalito.*

"We have *bachillerato trasnocheros trucos de
Apache y si nos agarran* in the U.S. of A they just
Send us across to our *frontera* suburban squatters.

"But ultimately *sabemos que Nuevo México,
Texas, California, Arizona y Colorado*
Are always *nuestras tierras.* We come-enter *a
Nuestro gusto, con ganas. Estas
Fronteras son mexicanas, de México, compadrito.
Ajúa, cholo, chale, ese no la chingues.
Canta, gallito* cross without concern
Nuevo México es terreno de Pancho Villa."

Mayanito

Way up there on top of clouds
Above the rain linkages
Western hemispheric mountains
Nearing heaven
Mayanito looking down
Observing rain below
Descending upon continental
Earth with generous showers . . .

Mayanito saddened that
Mountain clouds are not
Blessing him
Prayed to higher sources
Old civilizations
Centuries of rituals
Celestial spirituals . . .

Mayanito awakened in
Early morning with
Mighty gods united
Torrential warpath
Thundering warriors . . .

Mayanito's observed miracles
Gigantic raindrops
Landing powerfully
One by one
Nature's canopy
Like tiny soldiers
Bouncing briskly
Silent bombs plunging . . .

Mayanito in fields of eternity
Playing marbles rain *lluvia*
Drops dancing-n-marching
Joyfully rank-n-file
Newlyfound friends
Nature's *amigos*.

Sur Americano

Europeanismos genéricos piel de sociedades
Centro generaciones caudillistas /
Imperios militares exclusivos golpe de estados
Complejos indígena campesinos bajando sus
Pandillas reclamando años de opresión
La tierra potente de recursos la droga
Exclusiva adictiva el placer mundial controversial
Minerales esperando los hierros que penetren
Sus entrañas dándole luz a exclusiva clase alta
Millonarios base del hemisferio la segunda
Europa Española con cien dialectos de negros
Indígenas en contra punto de 27 dialectos
Españoles añádele el portugués los italianos
Alemanes integrados Inglaterra reclamando
El fútbol deporte importante fuerza
Mundialmente conocidos su música corazones
Pulpo de expresiones tango bonito boleros cumbias
Andinas vallenatos salseros pulmones bellezas
Mujeres aclamadas universo literatura al alto
Majestuoso se traduce sus luminas raíces
Inmediatamente a dar a luz guerrilleros campesinos
Institucionalizando nuevos estados armados
Océanos montañas todavía naturales la pobreza
Epidémica embajada de militantes revolucionarios
Visionarios abogando colores indígenas
Con cien dialectos regionales
Rodeando la exclusividad sociedades media
Alta intelectual avanzada distinguido desarrollo
Potencial cuando el dólar se convierta en pan
Americano sólo una moneda como Europa.

Puerto Rico's Chupacabras

Following confirmed researched sightings apparitions
Sanctioned hemispheric telescopers consortium
Galaxy study approved Milky Way council of
Strange phenomena P.O. Box 15 Jupiter Moon
Data cum da cum space planet X int. net Web site
Chupacalabrium council hijas de maría Venus
Chapter sighting's daily report.

Chupacabras is the following:

A mezcla-cockfight ducha boricua
Pulsars and quasars meteor showers
Ionosférico platillo volador radio
Signals linked Arecibo's Sinkhole
Observatory se estalló un cometa
Giving birth to an extra-terrestrial

"Déjate de cuentos, brother, yo lo vi
porque me lo contó mi abuelita que
masca tabaco y es medio ciega
sitting in her veranda at twelve o'clock
ella me bipeó en la celular she told me
that deep into el Yunque Rain Forrest
an international gathering of coquís
tired of being heard not seen
palpitated themselves into a frenzy
consortium orchestral symphonic
mellifluous acapellos y nació un fantasma."

"Qué sabes tú, mal educao, la chupacabras es
un acidic petro chemical pharmaceutical
residue illegally deposited blended arrabal
with an encountered Santería witchcraft
brujos by-the-sea espiritista demonic séance
es un trabajo del Diablo, sacúdete, satanás."

"Compañeros, vamos a llegar al cráneo intelectual
nuestra posición es la siguiente: in this Puerto
Rican island full of conflicts and political
indecisions the nation floating in listless circles
dando vueltas como el viejo carrusel
tuvimos un sueño colectivo empezamos
a halucinarnos en un estado esquinillazofrénico."

"Es que esos socialistas hablan y no se entiende
ni un comino, la pura realidad es que chupacabras
es un movimiento independentista
es un multi-party umbrella strategy
creating new medicinologies to supplant
the island research grants y ahora pagamos
peaje tres cincuenta por minuto en la internet
compañía nacionalista y Lolita Lebrón
la dueña del chupacabras Web site."

"Óigame, consorte, ven acá, déjame leerte las
barajas en mesa blanca págame cinco pesos
por la consulta los espíritus me dicen
que la chupa es un agente de la F.B.I.
que las cabras son AWACs surveillance
están documentando el nalgueo de los fundillos
de activistas buscando información
de los terroristas, cuídate."

"Esa gente está craqueá, que tú crees de eso
yo soy él y ella que camina las noches
en las barrancas buscando ambiente
yo soy director y directora de la farándula
let me tell you the real deal, la chupacabras
surgió de un Halloween costume party
lagartijos y lizards sapos transvestial hip-hop
dance psychedelic bisexual underground
rap mezcalinado pitorro moonshine
medical marijuana mixed with ecstasy
píldoras cocainadas mixed with one-hundred-

fifty proof ron Don Q disguised in one substance.
Si con eso no salió la cabra, tú no chupastes."

"Brother, lo que tú dijistes es una mentira total
¿vistes?, mi pana, en Puerto Rico no bebemos
el chupacabras is an organizational secret
Boricua password palabra secreta, mano
Borinquen hysteria vampiric mascota es un
equipo que juega doble en liga extra-terrestial."

"Pueblo, the Puerto Rican people are always
being duped, compañeros, después de un
análisis intenso hemos concluido que la
entre comillas 'chupacabras' is the, cito,
'commercialization imperialist relajo-joke'
end of cito, cito twice entre comillas 'is the
promotion of un nuevo trago para embabucarnos
mixed with cranberry orange juice
muy delicioso, sabes, served with Bacardi
vampire teeth flying en cualquier esquina
sponsored by el lumpen sector camera de
comercios chapter of unemployed teamster
piragüeros,' end of cito, cito twice."

"Cállate, zafao, vete a trabajar pa que me mantengas
el gallo cucurucú es el experto de media madrugada
no duermen me contaron que la chupacabras
es la revancha of the Puerto Rican national pitirre
tired of being depicted as a third-class pájaro
disguising itself."

"La esencia es que un espíritu ambulante
transcendental was touched by the divine
cuatro gold mine of jíbaro sentimientos
y adaptó a la isla, señores, no hay más ná."

"Yeah, right, yo soy el incrédulo
there's a chupacabras out there,

and Jesus Christ ascended into
heaven in a UFO, yeah, right."

"The ultimate reality dicen los chamaquitos
que es un cartoon superhero scaring nightmares
Walt Disney theme park production for the
Caribbean basin."

"Aquí lo que hay es un catálogo de tostaos,
yo soy la única religiosa que reza rosario
de la virgin maría en las iglesias pentecostales,
el chupacabras es la atalaya, the armageddon
is coming, el fin del mundo, es un invento
de los testigos de jehová para vender
periódicos en las esquinas."

"And me, too, nuyorican, bro, I'm chupacabras'
illegitimate nephew street-vendor pestering
you to purchase this t-shirt taped account
Kodak moment for $16.95 take five bolita
winning numbers, what a bargain!"

"Finalmente llegamos a la conclusión que el
chupacabras es el espíritu de Toño Bicicleta
protected from the authorities by the Puerto
Rican nation Toño celebrated his every escape
ritualistically drinking virgin goat blood
he killed them with two souvenir plastic
machetes like the Spanish toreadores who
beben sangre when they kill the toros
this document is sponsored by PETA's
Brigitte bear-all as God acknowledged
lo que habíamos percibido
que Puerto Rico es 100 x 35 x 1000
historias chupacabra folktales
breeding creatively nuestras mitologías."

Fronteras

Indigenous

stomp your feet
affirm you live
on stolen lands
native peace pipers
WAKAN God-sun
twenty-eight directions
worshipping earth's
sweat lodge
cleansing bird's
multi-tongue speakers

stomp your feet
to advanced civilizers
pow-wow heart drum
WACIPI feast
real estate owners
multi-trillion illegal
treaties hidden inside
university historical
municipality vaults
constitutionalizers
legal eagle vultures
hemispheric brutal
holocaust

stomp your feet
shout-out in demand
shout-out all at once
"give them their land
or give them reparation"

stomp your feet

Español

entonces out of our spiritual resolve
we began to create con tu diploma
apellido de la nada adentro de
rutas migratorias producción
de nuevas culturas
nuestras guaguas recogiendo
las frutas de tar-brea fría
en la migra los callos
are re-cycled en un cuero
duro tremendo bilinguazo
de pobreza nos abandonastes
nos vendistes, you sold us out.

ahora nuestra piel esquinillera
te adoba with palabras migrantes
en el hemisferio cross-roots fertilizing
sueños podridos stitched inside
singer machines.

now, we, gente de sangre gorda
metiéndole miedo a tu real academia
española cucándote con millones de
palabras continentales trabalenguas
enmixturadas cocinándose en asuntos
hemisféricos combinando lingüísticas
en proporciones humanas.

el español sagrado es una frontera jíbara
indígena con modismos dichos negristas
criollismos mitologías de melaza manteca
españolizada interlingüe con betún.

now the world anxiously awaits our noveleros
cuentistas poeteros modernistas armados con

lenguas multi-mixtas con crónicas documentando
we existed before we discovered colón.

el español sagrado sucursal de invasión de árabes y gitanos
experimentos enmixturados like the twenty-
seven dialectos you speak España conquistadora
you took the gold leaving us powerless
forcing our imperialistic caudillo struggles
to reconstruct your traditional European lengua
creating our western hemispheric tongue.

but alas i love you Spanish
half of my lengua
part of my tongue
i'm gonna fight for you siempre i am
your humble son
qué tragedia
qué contra
dic ci ón.

Tesis de Negreza

(canción de bobby capó)
(reseña del dr. víctor manuel vega)

"mataron al negro bembón"
negrito cocolo llamado prieto
alborazado blah blah blah

"mataron al negro bembón"
ambujo separación
indistinguida blah blah blah

"hoy se llora noche y día"
nos dicen que somos
calpa mulato iguales blah blah blah

"porque al negrito bembón"
cambujos somos unidos
en este hemisferio *chino*
no existe el racismo blah blah blah

"todo el mundo lo quería"
coartado burla insensitiva blah blah blah

"porque al negrito bembón"
chumbo pueblo antipatía blah blah blah

"todo el mundo lo quería"
churusco entonces pues:

"y llegó la policía"
cimarrón defensa raza alta bravía

"y arrestaron al matón"
sus labios *criollos* suculentos

"y uno de los policías"
moreno saboreando sus pupilas

"que también era bembón"
cocolo no la tengo escondida

"le tocó la mala suerte"
cuarterón está aquí mismita

"de hacer la investigación"
soy *emancipado* para que enrojezcas
con mis cachondos coloreados

"le tocó la mala suerte"
falucho sangre roja mezclada

"de hacer la investigación"
jíbaro de congoleses chupetes
labios de erección grandiosa

"y sabe la pregunta"
grifo montañas sutil dulzura

"que le hizo al matón"
ladino betunando emoción
borinqueñosos poros

"porque lo mató"
liberto temblor besos volcánicos
del cielo viniste y devolviste

"diga usted la razón"
manumiso internas calenturas

"y sabe la respuesta"
mestizo profundas entrañas

"que le dio el matón"
moreno rosando sus raíces:

"yo lo maté por ser tan BEMBÓN"
morisco le contesta
voy a sacar la lengua para limpiarte
de tus sutiles prejuicios

        "el guardia escondió la lengua y le dijo"
        soy *niche* para insultarte cuando me insultes
        para confrontarte cuando tu ignorancia
        desigualdad escupe estereotipos
        soy *lobo* voy a sacar la bemba patriótica
        colectiva humana cuando me respetes
        amistosamente

                "ésa no es razón"
                soy *loro* voy a sacar la bemba
                la que nunca había escondido

"para matar al bembón"
soy *mulecón* bemba enmelezada
con cien millones de negros
continentales

        "ésa no es razón"
        soy *muleque* marca de hierro
        caliente lacerado marca de *carimbo*

                "huye huye"
                soy *moyeto* aquí la segunda áfrica
                dividida por yemayá

                        "que ahí viene el matón"
                        soy *negro pardo* que se
                        aparezca el matón

                                "ésa no es razón"
                                soy *quinterón* lo confronto
                                con bembazo indigno

"yo te digo que viene"
soy *retinto* valiente ciudadano

"cortando bembas"
soy *saltoatrás* arresto
al criminal canalla

"ya se la cortó"
soy *tente en el aire*
investigo la letra de bobby capó
"al negrito bembón"
soy *torno atrás*
analizo la grabación
de rafael cortijo
los soneos dulce creativos
de ismael rivera
soy *zambaigo*
critico mi-tato-pecado
repito mil veces este folklore
"ésa no es razón"
soy *zambo* bemba escopeta
sacude bemba gloriosa
"esconde la bemba" nunca
mas soy un majestuoso
BEMBÓN.

Spanglish

pues estoy creando spanglish
bi-cultural systems
scientific lexicographical
inter-textual integrations
two expressions
existentially wired
two dominant languages
continentally abrazándose
en colloquial combate
en las aceras del soil
imperio spanglish emerges
control pandillaje
sobre territorio bi-lingual
las novelas mexicanas
mixing with radiorocknroll
condimented cocina lore
immigrant/migrant
nasal mispronouncements
baraja chismeteos social club
hip-hop prieto street salsa
corner soul enmixturando
spanish pop farándula
standard english classroom
with computer technicalities
spanglish is literally perfect
spanglish is ethnically snobbish
spanglish is cara-holy inteligencia
which u.s. slang do you speak?

Encimitadelinglés

encimitadelinglés, nené
apabullando sus tonalities
con el keeping-up
five hundred palabras
they invent every week

encimitadelinglés, nené
intimately touching
caressing her limb's existence
playing with her letras
manipulándola out of
her english-only
ignorancia

encimitadelinglés, nené

la
com
puta
dora
tenfingering me e-mailing me
under around underneath
her teclas
wet
me
mojo

into her micro-chips
into her macro-soft tela
into her hard wares
telecom-municating me
electrically wiring me
wet-me-mojo enfermito
soy cortejo of her
majestic spider
web-page-ness

estoy encimitadelinglés, nené

Bilingüe

exploring and dissecting
texto bilingüe
definiendo canción
nacional sylvia rexach
olas y arenas with
standard poetic spanglish

soy la arena
que en la playa está tendida
envidiando otras arenas
que le quedan cerca al mar
eres tú la inmensa ola
que al venir
casi me tocas
pero siempre
te devuelves hacia atrás
las veces que te derrama
sobre arenas humecidas
ya creyendo
que esta vez
me tocarás
al llegarme
tan cerquita
pero luego te recojes
y te pierdes
en la inmensidad
del mar

soy la arena
que en la playa está tendida
vive sola su penar
eres ola
que te envuelves
en la espuma
y te disuelves
en la bruma

a l e j á n d o t e m e m á s

finely grained crystals
sea-polished
weightless granules
in a sensual cocktail planted
smoothly naked grounds
cha-cha-turned sharp curves
palm tree spanglish figurines
inviting her olas y arenas
pasando my boricua hands
riding breezes
por tu open bosom
tidal waves mistress
tu luna yearnings
arriving madrugada's solemnity
pregnant many periods
virgin fragility

into my canela-brown sugar-
coated bomboncitos
melting deliciously . . .

allá in your open pores
i receive your luscious lips
buscándote borinquen
your cinnamon-powdered
tongue mi tierra
somos siete millones
en múltiples
fronteras lingüísticas

ya no nos cabe una sola lengua

Mixturao

(for English only)

we-who engage in
western hemispheric
continental spanish majority
communally sharing linguistics
in humanistic proportions

we-who integrate
urban America
simmering each other's slangs
indigenous nativizing
our tongues' cruising accents
who are you, English,
telling me, "Speak only English
or die."

we-who grassroots
and jíbaro dialectics
yodeling Mexican riddles
chicano "ese" talk
creole caribbeanisms
black negroid textings
african twisting
european colonizers'
oppressive repertoires
savoring new vocabularies
who are you, English,
telling me, "Speak only English
or die."

we-who create continental music
elaborate universal jazz
rhythmic tonalities
vallenato oilings
gospel-rap soulings
brazilian portuguesa
bonito bolero

mayan songs soothing
quebecois hard rock
patois saging
andino cumbias
world-wide tango curvings
merengue-calypso
mating-mixing dancing
tres por cuatro cubanities
con los pasos firmes de aztecas
who are you, English,
telling me, "Speak only English
or die."

we-who are at peace in continental
inter-mixtures
do hereby challenge
united states isolationism
anti-immigrant mono-lingual
constitutional bullets
declarations telling us to
"speak only english or die"
"love it or leave it"
spelling big stick carcass
translations universally excluded
multi-lingual multi-cultural
expressions "need not to apply"
who are you, English,
telling me, "Speak only English
or die."

so enter our multi-lingual
frontiers become a sharing
partner maybe then I might
allow you the privilege
to call me a tremendous
continental "MIXTURAO."

Mujeres

Riqueña Hip-Hop

yo
me
llamo
borincana
jíbara
puertorra
hermana
me
hinco
toda
en
mi
patria
su
estrella
alta
y
brava
anhelamos
ese
día
en
que
en
plena
carretera
bofeteamos
descarada
cantante
la madona
por arrastrar
sus nalgas
con nuestra
querida
bandera

Enrojo

(casi todos y todas . . . miramos . . . pensamos}

she walks . . .
pure
air
divinity
east
harlem
barrio corridors
old-fashioned
cartera
held-in
precious curvings
detalles her
espíritus
protectivos
jealously
guarding
"concho brother"
can't even
touch with words
she walks . . .
so I watched
disimulando from afar
curándome con luscious
adventurous
ashamed-of-myself
enfermito
picantes
calenturas
que me vengo
talking
thinking
por favor
cógeme "pena, nena"

hablando
on behalf of all
my continental
amigos in silence
tirando piropos
atoloquedá

Instrument

ivory heads patiently awaiting
countless encounters
daily tightening seductions
fragilities skin-tight lean
nude elegance
all ten fingers feeling up-n-down
they use her moon nocturnal cave
resonating her high peaks
mountain's serenity
resonating
her all-world pitches
they seduce her
she takes all
she wants more she inspires
she stands
deep cuts womb rituals
erection's ecstasy
they proclaim her "la reina de mil nombres"
they acclaim her "the queen of a thousand names"
they undress her ivory petals
they loosen her thin-veiled
see-through nightgown
they encase her velvet smooth blanket
they crown her "tierra"
they call her land "land"
ultimate adulation
"diosa gitana"
        "gypsy goddess"
                "la guitarra"
                        they call her
                                "the guitar"

Milenio

confetti of lágrimas
fantasy tears
landing in san juan manhattan
perfection placed
elegantly sculptured
puerto rican ambiguities
infinite space tears
gotas tearing like
warm church bells-campanitas
new year millennium
past, present, future
lágrimas all in one
effervescent moment
año viejo aguinaldos
despedida tears
choral singing
lustfully auld lang syne
año nuevo
nueva vida
twelve o'clock
las doce celebration
bohemian champagne
poetic brindis
future altar
la danza boricua
dancing libertad
still an añoranza
restless and powerless
cadre confetti of lágrimas
warm gotas raining
like composer rafael hernández
snow flakes melodic tribute
"tilín tilín tilán" landing
softly this new millennium
entering my yet-to-be resolved
political status

Tumbadora

(canto)

faithful roots tu noble base	tu cum
quinto tiempo landing clave	tu cum cum cum
repicando snapping fingers	tu cum cum cum
armonioso sonero cantar	tu cum
historias tu diosa alabar	tu cum
aquí es que sale el coro	tu cum
prenda preñada	tu cum
cuidando tus loros	tu cum
folclores tesoros	tu cum
caja fuerte que preserva	tu cum
valores africanos	tu cum
sacudiéndote te relajas	***tu cum pru cu tum tum tum***
piel madre la base mulata	***tu cum pru cu tum tum tum***
cuba respire tus pupilas	***tu cum pru cu tum tum tum***
caribe urbaneada	cum
espiritista madama	cum
potencia boricua	cum
nos lleva la clave	cum
reina de las llaves	cum
despojamos	cum
oye bailamos	cum
el coro y el pueblo	cum
gloriosas caderas	cum
long live	***pru cu tum tum tum***
long live	***pru cu tum tum tum***
long live	***pru cu tum tum tum***
	tum tum
	tum tum
	tum tum
	hail our majesty
	touch tumbadora
	our QUEEN!

Hombres

Spanglish Carta

(to José Luis González)

In the fondo of a new york city blackout
i read your stories time
and
time again dos negritos cucándome
mi búsqueda allá adentro
en el bajo hundido manhattan
papote sat on the stoop
en el bajo hundido fanguito
melodía gateaba su famoso baquiné.

Arrabal impressions urban
barrio che che colé puente-bridge
crossing from 106th street
boulevard a cuadras de la universidad
de puerto rico todos miramos into el
botecito martín peña filthy infested
alleluia waters spermed putrid residues
comiéndose y tragándose sunday
garbage impuridades absorbiéndose
totalmente condená a muerte
buscando an illusion como cristo
reflections three days old
una melodía se asoma en el fondo
el estomaguito soon to be filled with
aperitivos of waste.

El negrito se asoma
al caño órgano de sonidos
se entrega looking for dance
plena boat en el miedo del caño
at the center an addiction
in martín peña death cursing
from his grave "quién diablos
dio mi nombre a esta gran miseria"
no salty piñones alcapurrias
no luquillo beach jueyes
no el yunque service road pasteles

melodía papote eating nada
comiendo impurities velloneras
screams firecrackers cuerpecito
swimming drowning debajo la
tierra fanguito de borinquen
what a lovely national treasure
infected with negreza ambulante
la miseria ate him up
la patria no lo rescató no se asustó
de este descaro of all ages
ni agueybaná ni los españoles
ni los espíritus prietos se compadrinaron
papote sat on the stoop
melodía solamente lives
inside puerto rican folklore
borinquen se esconde
mientras que el negrito gulp gulp
tragaderos for patches in the asses
melodía gulp gulp gulps estereotipos
patria somos culpables
melodía soy negrito tres veces
vaccinated in lengua prieta
negroide mulatto of no stars
spanglish ebonic disparatero
physical expressions linguistically
crippled with no skies ahorcado
en el fondo fundillo del hoyo fango
clay urinadero no room to breathe
fósiles arqueológicos
sancocho cacadero
eating sopa de microbios
papote sat on the stoop
negrito melodía cocolo prieto
molleto desaparecido infierno
trabalengüero misinformed
blown-up hijo of advanced insularism
melodía papotes descalzos on stoops
of an abandoned nationhood

José Luis González hundió a melodía
en su fondo me fui a buscarlo
read him twenty times upon
the first encounter
me compadrinastes
my creative fuentes born
y poetic dialogue accelerated
como novio en el altar i awaited
your latest pronouncements
to masticate into your phrasings
even then siempre nos cucabas
criticisms of my non-linguistic nada
non-validating me
are you a crucible?
how many reseñas discursos
classroom discussions phd positional
papers inspiring careers with your
marxist pronouncements
from mexican exilio philosophically
advanced universal polemics
national implants
managerial utopias
país de cuatro pisos excluding
papote-melodías
fraternities of humanity.

But you inspired us into
penhood introspection
and we bestow upon you
an african chegüigó
Don José Luis González
reminding you that
en el fondo del nuyorican
definitivamente
hay un puertorriqueño.
Gracias.

Patriota

(to Clemente Soto Vélez)

when i think of Clemente Soto Vélez
i think of an ecumenical document
patriotic humanity

when I think of Clemente Soto Vélez
i think of a social treatise
specialized dignity
ambassadorial leadership
ultimate beso compañero

when i think of Clemente Soto Vélez
i think of camaraderic affection
of his companion AMANDA
Clemente's center of all

when I think of Soto
illuminating wordsmith
carefully crafting
every letter
chiseling harmonious sounds
molding syllables
shaping words
creating images
bursting streaming
consciousness
directing us into
introspection

when I think of Vélez
i think of total independencia
incarcerated militant
la princesa prison
la masacre de ponce

lifetime faithful patriota
passionate speaker
"Qué Viva Puerto Rico Libre"
de cualquier manera in any form
"patria o muerte se lo juro, venceremos."

Militant

brothers and sisters, do you want to witness
a virus that is not found in the computer
just take a look at the lifetime breeding
hoodlums daily initiating a mental rape
selling perdition protection ruthless
cowards they are after our community's
health waiting for our children in the
stairs of your streets selling them protection
from sidewalk destiny they use your
weakneses forcing young souls into
drugs criminality offering death scholarships
they infuse inject you with high-powered
certificates methadoning children of early
childhood they create a climate diversion
of fear holding young people hostage
with sedatives enlarging teenage minds
recruiters company prizes best salesperson
of empty dreams lost lives they collect
weekly bonuses for most deformities
in the eyes of our avenues daily we witness
them preying the housing complexes
stationed outside emergency rooms, walk-in
clinics, drugstores, pharmacies offering
painkillers binoculars looking for children
in the school playground community
bodega outpost for those who lack lunches
outside sneakers blockbuster stores wishes
with 3 dollars rent a movie one day free
beeper use instamatic cellulars hip-hop
jeans styled consumerism pressures
they provide the goods for teenagers to achieve
material dreams big-timing our children's
illusions while our social club sellers of
sunday liquor and church service all of us

the rest guilty we watch them washing our
hands like pontius pilate the devil satanic
bandits we blame society social criminal
penal systems our inabilities to confront
the vultures destroying our future.

Consignas in Brutality

(shout outs for Anthony Báez)

"once again discrimination
blatantly upon our nation . . ."

no justice, no peace, el silencio nos mata aquí

they shoot us, they club us,
they kill us, they choke us,
open prey to murder, coro

no justice, no peace, el silencio nos mata aquí

let's protect our community borders

no justice, no peace, el silencio nos mata aquí

they give justice to police aggressors
courts and judges give them protection

no justice, no peace, el silencio nos mata aquí

show our rage, show our face
demand justicia all the way

no justice, no peace, el silencio nos mata aquí

hear the cry, hear the cry,
unfair verdicts, unfair trials
credible witnesses need not apply

no justice, no peace, el silencio nos mata aquí

let's shout out, let's shout out

"now everyone together"
"let's sing and march together"

“this is a defining moment”
“total victory we mutter”
“let’s demand our civil rights”
“children/people must not die”

no justice, no peace, el silencio nos mata aquí

Trueno . . . Relámpago . . . Lluvia . . . Nieve . . .
Aquí . . . Estamos . . . Unidos . . . Soldados . . .
En Lucha . . . Presente . . .

no justice, no peace, el silencio nos mata aquí
no justice, no peace, el silencio nos mata aquí

Preludio Barroquero

(para Luis López Adorno)

crítica de un concierto para desobedientes
doce años in fermenting adagios
sutiles de la patria allegro palabras
andantes parábolas criollos morales
principled religious mythologies
puerto rican parodies eclectic
inquietudes de carretera voluptuoso
caribe's studious inclusions of
quevedo sílabas imagist ezra pound
mirones jack agüero sonnetic
exactness letras al gorete
palesianismos con ánimo español
24 cenizas ana lydia vega zealotry
guardianship beloved Spanish
language expanded a un espíritu
scherzo excomulgado rompiendo
el puro aire clásico palabras
puntiagudas ángel luis méndez
anclas con la muerte en el insomnio
irregular-shaped perlas del caribe
anti-social opposition ambiguous
imageries powerful tensions
flotando en el sub-current aguada
grotesca de cerro gordo this
anti-desconcierto island adorno
rapture-ruptured symphony
obedient dientes de
aliteraciones verbos musculares
ultimate contradictions enchantments
how can you stage a concert
para desobedientes expect anarchy
tumultuousness verbal abuse

expect schizophrenia
expect tomatoes political insurrection
expect social insubordination
adorno destroys and constructs
desobediencia la pava's ultimate
orchestral concierto based in nada?

Carpetas in Your Dossier

(para Ramón Bosque Pérez)

walking slowly like the jehovah witnesses
armed with intelligence instruction
they quietly dispersed into all avenidas
boulevards streets and callejones basements
to collect information cia fbi speculators
builders disguised next to you this noche
of every day helicopters high tech chips
in your dossier salieron como hormigas
of all ethnic varieties and moved into el pueblo
gentrification taking place protect your rentas
blowing up cerquillos los building cranes
skyscrapers on 96, 97, 98 streets food emporiums
on 110th street salieron at 2 o'clock
in the morning out of a secret community
meeting place smelling your underwear
investigating vieques peaceful patriotas
mexicanos ilegales arabic suspects
so open your ojos into a citizen's arrest
los trucos agresivos of intelligence
nos-vigilan-ten cuidao
they transform como las sombras
tienen "control" of two thousand
venas through your pores
nos inyectan por los radio waves
limpiando los cocos con seductive
material conocen that-they-know
el paradero de tus besos secretos
and intimate ten-cuidao
ellos instalan the cable system
al oído de tus nalgas te-lo-juro
that we live en un estado
inconsciente de temor

los awac surveillance supervise y analizan
los granos de arroz that you eat
nos tienen fichao they know
nos tienen embabucao saben
tus mínimos fallos encelulao
tienen cien maneras
to kill you frame you and matarte
they have thousands of agents informers
your most intimate amigo detailing
all your detalles stored in microchips
american scrambled jeringonza
radio micro waved signals
nos tienen limping in circles
desbalanceados with uncertainties
targeted en las entrañas del net-web
lavado de cerebro impeding
your conciencia con un candao of steel
armed with invisible keys
targeting our cultural centers
into ritzy private ownership
tattooing into our schizophrenia
abre los ojos no cojas miedo
ármate with all your resources
ten cuidao

Vecindario

Callejerismos

ÓYEME lenguas comunitarias no me eches
la culpa yo soy una simple recogedora bochinchosa
comentando libremente todo lo que tú sabes
no te atreves a decir públicamente pero lo
hablas privadamente así que tranquilo
no saques cuchillas ni me des mal de ojo
no me culpes ni me lleves a la corte
no me acuses de estereotiparlos
como insensitiva pero la lengua que
no es mía comentando que los cubanos
y sus amigos puristas como Jerry Gonzales
el trompetista siempre con la misma vaina
y que Cuba es el centro de la salsa pero
los puertorriqueños son los mejores
arreglistas han mantenido la salsa por
muchos años también son la universidad
de soneros salvaron la salsa como Frankie Ruiz
suave nueva música raíces farándula amor
con percusión ÓYEME Rubén Blades
trató y que un crossover con lírica de nueva
canción para ser actor y abogado para perder
las elecciones de panamá pero concho todavía
es el compositor número pedro navaja nos
hace falta su combinación con Willie Colón
todos sabemos que el merengue es el baile
preferido en los salones de baile en Puerto Rico
existe un catálogo de bochinches se coge
la noche entera El Canario dando
complaint que la puertorriqueña Olga Tañón
se gana los Emmy dominicanos muchos no
saben que los Mambo Aces Roberto Roena
fueron los primeros en hacer coreografía con
los coristas no se apuren que yo soy equal

opportunity comentadora de las novelas
mexicanas lloronas con actores de quinta clase
todos tienen guilles de cantante de sexta categoría
pero la Thalía la que se casó con Mottola
el jefe de Sony Records la que se quitó dos
costillas y tiró bomba por visitar a la diva
María Félix en el cementerio sin conocerla
está en Nueva York para competir
con la diva absoluta number one J Lo
personalmente los boricuas acusan a Celia Cruz
por no apoyar a Andy Montañez porque los
cubanos de Miami no lo dejaron cantar
porque él visitó a Pablo Milanés en Cuba por
eso es que Gloria Estefan no canta en Puerto Rico
todos sabemos que la mejor salsa del mundo
se baila por los Puerto Ricans en Orchard Beach
pero el merengue es el baile
número uno de Latinoamérica simplemente
porque uno nace bailando merengue no hay
que quitar los pies de la pista ÓYEME pero
la balada pop esa y los nuyorican raps se ganan
los Emmy platinum como Ricky nenudo partido yo
no entiendo cómo Santana se hace millonario
con la canción de Tito Puente "Oye Cómo Va" cuando
los mexicanos ni los chicanos no saben bailar
cha-cha-chá pero Selena la del tex-mex era la
más chula del mundo ésa tenía capacidad de
competir con la J Lo los nuyorican bailan
como los prietos los chicanos son indios pero
no bailan los dominicanos bailan
salsa a lo izquierdo no vamos a Washington
Heights a bailar merengue toda la boring noche
pero los boricuas no tienen ni un hit de bomba y
plena en la radio pero su gran folklore
sigue sobreviviendo en las paradas, la calle, el colegio y el hogar

la bachata compite con la salsa y el tex-mex
Juan Luis Guerra el rey de los estudiantes universitarios
hasta el presidente del colegio salió bailando
el dichoso merengue ÓYEME callejerismos así
por el estilo perdónenme pero como no tengo
show de radio ni televisión tengo que hablar ligero
y atoloquedá sintonícense mañana en cualquier
esquina para el próximo comentario de la gran
no-tengo-la-lengua-escondida la fabulosa ÓYEME,
por favor cómprenme este tape por veinte pesos.

El Difunto

Oye-yeow I'm not entering my compadre's
Funeral ni con dos escopetas
Amarradas inside my pantaletas

padre

De mis bolsillos not even with
Siete velas potencias con cuatro brujos

nuestro que

En mis esquinas haciendo hechizos
Oye-yeow I'm not going inside to see

estás

El difunto

en

Yeah, from outside in this corner
Look at Ms. Exquisita like she calls
Herself the loving daughter

los

La prima de la madrastra
Guillándose de ser hija postiza

cielos

She comes for the first time in two años
She lives around the corner

santificado

Si a llorar semejantes embustes

sea

She comes a buscar las maletas
Que el difunto guardaba

tu nombre

She rented that black dress
From the salvation army

vénganos

She painted false lágrimas
Como en las novelas

tu reino

La diablita arrived wearing
Un traje red escotao

hágase

She was dancing metal rock
En cbgb all night long

tu voluntad

Y qué sorpresa she claims to be
La única hija legítima

aquí

Del difunto

en la tierra

She was not a bastard
She claimed the maletas

como en el

Belonged to her the rightful heir

cielo

Y las dos se agarraron
Tooth and nail at the front
Door of the funeral parlor
All these cuernos accusations

el pan nuestro

The immigrant priest attempted
To separate them but his
Spanish was unintelligible his
English was non-existent
He sounded like a pre-recorded
Message while demanding
Extreme unction advanced payments

de cada día

El hermano Eusebio ex-ministro
Of five dollar mail-order reverendo
Licencia re-married with la botella

dánoslo hoy

He was praying with a manguera
Of bacardi emerging from
El baúl de su carro

y perdona

Oye-yeow te lo digo que Manny
El prestamista que dio el
Down payment

nuestras deudas

Until the social security
Releases veteran's insurance
That will arrive in five years

así como

Manny quiere cobrarle personalmente
A la viuda desamparada que está
Completa

nosotros perdonamos

La viuda with a daughter
Another born out of
Cuernos y los veinte gatos
So-called socios of gambling
Pesetas who brought
The pawn shop guy
To seize up el difunto's
Gold-filled tooth-melted
Payment of his debts

a nuestros deudores

Oye-yeow not me yo no
Entro allá adentro ni con
Secret service bodyguards

no nos dejes caer

The only decent group
Son las viejitas rosary specialists
But they do ten daily visits
Pray too fast and cannot be heard

en la tentación

Oye-yeow that's why I stay
Aquí outside afuera directing
El difunto's last will testament

mas líbranos

Please close the coffin and the
Ataúd as soon as the doors are
Opened no quiero ver ninguna
De estas chaviendas

del mal

That's why I stay outside
En el passing time de pasando
Tiempo, oye-yeow, compadre,
Descansa en paz

amén

Social Talk

Panamericanismo
Con qué se come eso
Pues es un pana amigo de América
Es un pan de revoltillo ham & eggs
No lo toques brother, eso es
Comunismo castrista in disguise
Te van a velar
Panamericanism
Son los Knights of Columbus italiano
Offshoot national holiday para
Amerigo Vespucci
Algo que tiene que ver con los
Prietos de África en el Caribe
Es un bakery americano en el
East Village
Un movimiento de universidades
For the lecture circuit
Pan es bread de América pero qué
Diablo es un nism ten cuidao eso
Tiene raíz de socialism te van a velar
Es el nuevo airline de Pan Am
Un movimiento de lingüistas aburridos
Las naciones unidas food stamps
O algo por el estilo
Una escuela de parachutes
Una boring palabra
No es un hit.

Harlem Elder Odes

They walk never afraid of shadows
They emerge unscathed
They turn corners
Verbal disputes toned down
Criminals pay respect
Cooling violent differences
They emerge unscathed
Those who dare to hurt them
Some say will become
Undocumented statistics
Inside coffin city morgue . . .

How tenderly sweet antique walk
Precious history broad exuberant
Smile children's kisses jumping
Tenderly into grandpa's loving arms . . .

From far away we prepare to greet
Them in awe of dignified charisma . . .

Clappings elevated alleluia praying
Breaking speed of sound gutting
Heaven's soul god's lord spirit

Choral harmony finger snapping
Hands celestially fathering black love . . .

Gospels entrenched down there
Clamoring rooted in slavery
Digging way down Lord Jesus
High-pitched spirituals sermonized
Drum songs polished souls . . .

They pray devoutly thanking God
Protecting Harlem from physical danger

Transcending church walking home
They spread God's blessings
Silent reverence anointed ambassadors
Peace for all . . .

Soul-good cooking fermented elder's hands
Old-fashioned recipes mathematically
Proportioned orally passed down
Devoured sugar yam pies crusting
Ivory teeth conservative Baptist
Elements "oooming" culinary reviews
Meticulous table manners surrendering
Temporary licking license marvelously
Embellished supported by Jesus
Granting sermon's delay to give
Almighty God enough time to
Resurrect eating out of his second
Soul food plate . . .

We talk our outrage
They quietly listen
We criticize
They remain expressionless
We accuse
They say nothing
They guru-listen
So let's repeat what has been
Said many times
One never knows what we have
Until we lose them
Don't take them for granted
Cherish them respect them
Honor the elder who taught you . . .

Innocence (to 9/11)

The day the U.S. lost its innocence,
was a cruel September 11, 2001
historical massacre.

The World Trade Center,
marketed as one acre per floor,
had no central steel beams
supporting its 220 stories.

A devastating mega-bomb,
filled with 157 human atoms,
aboard 2 domestic planes penetrated
the Twin Towers' ready coffins.

A devil cauldron, plotted
with synchronized exactness,
a maliciously curved winged
poisonous dart, aerial death ballet,
plunged the United States under fire,
wounds of war, life in living horror,
paralyzing the world and national psyche.

New York City is in a state of raw war.
Manhattan Island, a battleground zero,
confetti of tears, cemetery of candles,
poster tributes, wall-of-respect collages,
beloved photographs, community hand-
printing urgent requests, carved in paper
stones, outpouring of naked sadness,
looking for miracles, rescue turned to
recovery and removal, ash-laden carnage,
evaporated humans, particle remnants
of 1,000,000 body parts.

Metropolis broken hearts, scars of destruction,
cadre of humanity, healing laments,
consoling souls, army of volunteers,
red cross, blood, food, water, supplies,
counseling armed with prayer-peace,
God's potent weapon, we became
a collective consciousness of one.

Kudos to reflective patriotic and religious music,
parade of family and friends,
triumphant mayor, firefighters,
New York's finest, rescue workers
awarded golden heavenly medals.
A new era of working-
class simple patriots were
supplanting Hollywood's caricatures.
New York skyline a postcard odorous
Wall Street stench death-smoke
companion to Lady Liberty.

We will hold ourselves accountable
for maximum monetary payments
to afflicted families of this national
holocaust.

Perpetrators murdered over
3,000 civilians point blank!
This conspiracy, many years
in the making, map surveillance,
central planning, training, execution,
went unprotected by millions of
defense taxes that we pay.
Massive failure of intelligence services.
Our technology was blinded.
National security devoid of human
informant elements.

Vigorously we now investigate
the military architects of this brilliant insanity,
beyond the usual suspects,
who targeted 4 rockets into the
nerve of our political, military,
economic and civic establishments.

Innocence nevermore!
Our homeland liberty's enchantment
was peace in pieces
molesting ultimate freedoms.
The maiden was exterminated
by virile rugged villians
who loosened America the beautiful
for spacious skies celibate girdles,
who blindfolded her amber waves
of grain immaculate chastity.

Innocence nevermore!
America, home of the brave,
her unblemished naiveté
strapped and strangled,
her national couch
of security abandoned.
All-American wrestlers,
super bad athlete dudes,
hot-shot rally around "U.S.A. U.S.A."
were not alerted by the
organizations that protect us.
They could not protect the Madonna.
Our nuclear AWAC surveillance
pinned by 19 men of doom
sultans' box-cutter blades,
slingshot Davidians leveling
Goliath superpower supremacy
into countrywide submission.

The national flag shredded
in convulsions trembled fears.

Now the nation must flex its muscles,
endowed with world and papal approval
to punish the masterminds,
surrender them to justice,
dead or alive, patriotic cries,
military vengeance!

We are attacked as opulent abrasive infidels.
We are denounced as enemies of
World Order.
We are accused of fracturing ethical
traditional behavior.
We are exporting erotic sexual shamelessness in
the veils of traditional
world beliefs.
We are partisan to Israel.
We must abandon the Persian Gulf.

But we democratically reform our ways
in civilized governance.
We also respond to self-humanity, caring,
sharing, protecting, advising the world.
We have a million counter answers to
your accusations.
We discuss them in civilization.
We don't subject human society as
participants in your sacrifices.

Holy war now jihad emerging once again.
West against no-name nation.
U.S.A. at war with
invisible formidable untraditional
warfare units, highly disciplined,

military-educated logisticians,
cellular networks, anonymous donors,
armed with a martyrdom cell,
unrepentant in ending innocent lives.

Now we close ranks to our borders,
expired visas, deportations our resolve.
Liberty's shores closed the day
our civilians were bombed.
Terrorists implanted psychological
military presence,
acupunctured nerves of patriotism,
aroused suspicion, prejudice,
profiling mistrust.

Living cells in your middle-class
community waiting to unleash
anthrax explosive havoc and mistrust.
We are common suspects
of our daily outings,
strip-searched, detained
rampant fear haunting our
central nervous systems.

We will investigate e-mail
transactions of speculators
cowards who bought insurance
kissed our cheeks and
slashed our throats.

We must not become
vigilantes and discriminators.
Koran Muslim religion is
embellished in love and peace.
Allah, all-knowing, all-powerful,
all-merciful, all-faithful

categorically rejected
terrorists' final prayers.
Muhammad, the great prophet,
never will condone such
blatant and destructive
irresponsibility.

The nation demands:
leadership of unquestionable stature,
leadership versed in the etiquette
of world linguistics,
ambassadorial negotiators,
multi-strategists,
leadership that steers us
into just and peaceful
resolutions to this
long-term conflict
we confront.

We must negotiate with world maturity.
Let's stop this hemorrhage
that achieved its highest expectations!
If you don't close quarters for terrorists,
we will democratically or militaristically
support your opposition.
Counseled to be patient we are impatient.
tooth for tooth, person for person,
city for city, country for country,
we are on alert to destroy you!

The world is responsible to
address this human cry.
The world must protect itself.
Relentlessly we negotiate
anti-war resolutions from
committed nations.

Time is short. 62 countries
lost citizens in the rampage.

Yet our nation must transcend
conventional expectations.
But we demand justice!
Explain your irrational destruction
before the eyes of humanity!
Terrorist you are called!
That's your permanent label!
How beautiful your name!
Explain the ashes of destruction!
Over 3,000 body bags are empty and waiting!
You attacked the world, not the West!
You targeted your vile gutter warrior
misinterpretation of your sacredness!
You gained no friends, even in hell!
Educate us to the rationalization
of your vicious impotence!
There's no time to enter into negotiations!
Pay the world justice sentence
of your vicious crime!
Reform your hatred!
For our children's sake!
For your children's sake!
In the name of all!
In the name of Allah!
In the name of God!
Love knows no compromise!
Love knows no compromise!

Also by Tato Laviera

AmeRícan

Enclave

La Carreta Made a U-Turn

Mainstream Ethics